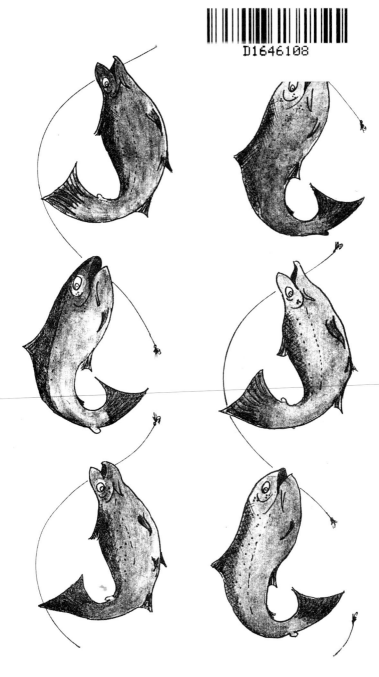

Thè Funny Sidè öf Salmon Fishing

The Böök öf Fishing Sènsè & Nönsènsè

Writtèn ånd illüstråtèd by Bill Bèwick

Bridge Studios
Northumberland
1989

ACKNOWLEDGEMENTS

To Arthur Temple who has fished for salmon on the Tweed for forty-five years and first took me salmon fishing twenty years ago, which has cost me a fortune ever since.

To the late Eric Robb, a superb gillie on the Spey who taught me to fish with small flies and to have fun on the water.

To the many friends, both male and female, I have met at the river who make life worth living and fishing all the more fun.

First published in Great Britain in 1989

by Bridge Studios
   Kirklands
   The Old Vicarage,
   Scremerston
   Berwick upon Tweed
   Northumberland TD15 2RB
   Tel: 0289 302658/330274

ISBN 1 872010 10 5

Typeset by EMS Phototypesetting, Berwick upon Tweed.

Printed in Great Britain by Martins of Berwick

To my wife Anne, who for years has put up with fishing holidays, dried my clothes, after I have fallen in, kept my fishing kit updated, washed my smelly socks, bought me old and new books on fishing, made food and provided drinks – and all done with never a single complaint.

FOREWORD

More people go fishing than go to football matches and so far there has been no suggestion of identity cards for water access although if poaching increases much more, cards and turnstiles may be required at each river. For the novice or newcomer to angling there is a whole range of tackle, technicalities, permits and rules to grapple with and initially they appear to be extremely baffling. Misunderstandings can be very embarrassing.

Like everything else in life, experience is essential and no book can ever outdo the knowledge to be gleaned at the water. A few days tuition on casting is also invaluable and worth a great many books. It is essential that you enjoy your fishing. It should be a pleasant day out, despite the weather and the conditions; my only real advice is that at all times you should retain your sense of humour and that is what this fishing book is all about. For there is more to fishing than catching fish.

CONTENTS

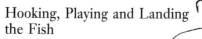

 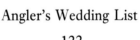

Without these Men, Wives, Birds, Fish, Animals and
Mermaids, this book would have been absolutely
impossible

Doctor Fisherfax

Willie The Gillie

WILLIAM - WILLYAM - WEELUM - WULL - WULLAY - WULLIE

KING *of* FISH

The salmon's abstinence from feeding in the river does not apply to drink.
That is why we find so many food trolleys and empty bottles in the water

UNDERSTANDING THE LIFE CYCLE OF THE SALMON

 HE basic life-cycle of the salmon is reasonably well understood and micro-tagging, tracking by radio and modern science is solving more of the mystery of this astonishing fish. However, some bits of its life-cycle have not been solved and I hope they never will.

Why does a salmon take a fly or a bait when it does not feed in fresh water?
How does a salmon find its way back to its native river?
What is the life-style and the whereabouts in the sea of smolts when they leave the river?

These are still largely unanswered questions. There are many species of salmon, but for our purposes we need only be concerned with the Atlantic salmon (*Salmo salar*), unless one of those others that look like the Hunchback of Notre Dame happens to stray into your river. The salmon starts its life as an egg in the river gravel spawning beds, called redds. In the months of late October, November and December the hen fish deposits many thousands of eggs in a series of holes dug out with her tail. The eggs are then fertilised by the randy cock salmon releasing its sperm (milt) over the eggs. Incidentally, salmon parr are also known to like a dabble in this ritual. The hen fish then proceeds to cover the eggs with gravel – a bit like a burial only no one is standing around waiting for grave-digging tips. Further graves will be required as most of the cock fish die from the excitement of the orgasm, as do many of the hen fish from such a boring sex life. The eggs hatch out in about two or three months provided they are not silted up or eaten up. At this stage they are called alevins and have an unfortunate start in life with a sac hanging around their necks. If they manage to get rid of the sac these baby salmon turn into fry and to save themselves from getting into the fat, start producing a camouflage system, which looks like fingerprints, down each side of their bodies. This is not caused, as many think, by anglers who forget to wet their hands while gently removing them from hooks to return them to the river. It is illegal to take fry, just in case you fancied trying a new line on whitebait, but unfortunately the law does not apply to the wildlife. The fry are very popular with predators, which thoroughly enjoy a fry-up, and will help themselves to large numbers. Brown trout have a great liking for this feast. No wonder, in later life, they turn into cannibals. Having survived all that, the little salmon now becomes a parr. Parr for the course is about twenty-four months but can vary from sixteen to forty-eight depending on the conditions in which the small salmon has to play and how many points it scores. You might say parr marks. If the parr is any good and about six inches long it is then presented with a silver finish, given a handicap and called a smolt. The smolts can then be heard reciting Masefield's 'I must go down to the sea again . . .' which they do. In fact they have no choice, for the river supermarkets do not have enough food to support such a large fish population. The smolts, if they can dodge the sea predators, such as seals and other fish, reach the rich delicatessens around Greenland where Weight Watchers do not have a branch and thus put on an enormous amount of weight. Some fish get fed up with all this eating and decide to come home within twelve months. These are called grilse. A few get lost and end up in the wrong house, which is not surprising considering the lack of river direction signs. Other fish may stay away for two to four years before coming home. Both cock and hen fish returning to their home rivers for the first time are called maidens which, when you think about it, is a little confusing as only hen fish can be virgins. Like many maidens they can vary in weight from a young wench of 10lb to a mature fish of 30-40lbs and sometimes they become right old bags or baggots if they don't spawn at all. When a salmon does come back – and this can be at various times throughout the year – it has a nasty habit of bringing lice with it; fortunately it loses them after being in the river about forty-eight hours. Salmon are called springers in the spring and backenders in the autumn. This does not mean that autumn fish are gay (although they do change their silver dress-colours to a shade of red). The fish then pair up at the redds; the hen fish starts to dig while the cock watches – just like humans – and the whole cycle starts again. The fish that survive spawning are called kelts and can be heard singing on their way down river, 'Here we go again'.

PRINCE CHARLIE.

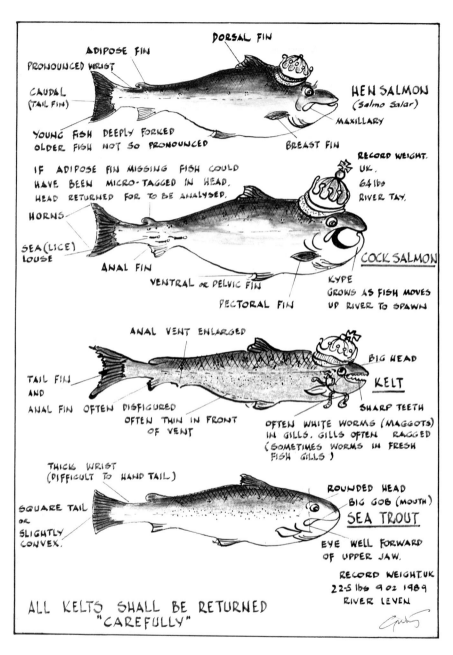

Kelts can look well-mended and silver in colour. They often get killed by inexperienced anglers through lack of observation and knowledge

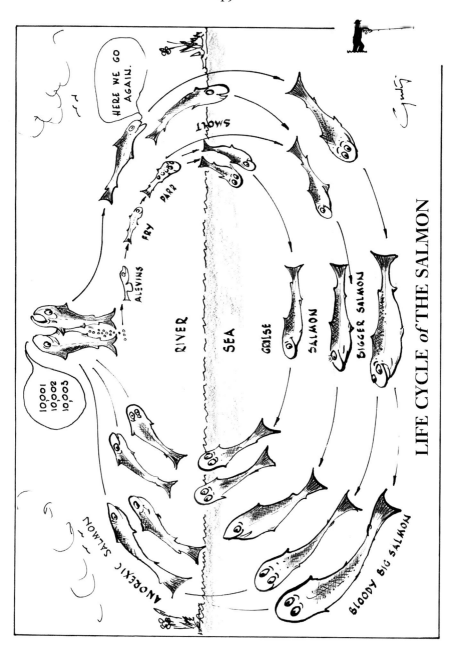

LIFE CYCLE of THE SALMON

Check list – All you need for a day's fishing

An angler at Upper Dalkeith
Ate haggis with curried old beef
But in bushes did find
He'd left the loo roll behind
But thanked God for the old docken leaf

The advantages of using a check list before going fishing

Always check your tackle – you have done all the jobs required. This is best done the night before you go fishing.

Poor casting is not the only reason for not catching fish

"A SALMON LEAP."

Bright day – Bright fly. Dull day – Bright fly.
Dull day – Dull fly. **Bright day** – Dull fly.

You don't often catch moving fish – salmon resting in their lies give the best chance. Recognise lies. Both water and fisherman's

A gillie who knows the beat is worth his weight in whisky – sometimes

"Aa! BUT ITS A GRAUND DAY FOR THE FISHING SIR"

Boats can be dangerous – if in doubt don't go out

Rivers are dangerous – look out for leaves, wood and twigs floating down river – often the first sign of a flood or rising water. Put in a stick-marker.

There is growing concern about salmon farming and the effect it may have on the wild fish population.

"CLEAN RUN FISH"

A first aid kit is often required at the water including hook-cutting pliers

Salmon run rivers all the year round. Do your homework when booking fishing

They say dog owners look like their dogs. What about gillies?

THE ROD

HE rod is the most essential piece of tackle when catching fish, unless you are a poacher. It has four basic functions:

To get the bait or lure to the fish.

To manipulate the bait or lure when in the water.

To play and hopefully land the fish.

To keep the tackle shops and manufacturers off the dole.

Seventeenth and eighteenth century rods were of one piece with a line fixed at the top and made from ash and cobnut hazel. This led to the angler's greeting on a cold day of 'How's your nuts?' Sectional rods came into fashion in the late nineteenth century. Like women, rods come in all sizes, shapes and lengths. You should buy two rods to start with. A fly rod and a spinning rod. The quality of the rods you buy will depend on the state of your bank balance. Again, like women, rods have different actions; hard or soft.

Select a rod with great care for it is more critical than choosing a future wife or mother-in-law. If possible try one for action at the water side (the rod not the mother-in-law). Before acquiring a rod consider these three options:

Buying New
This keeps the tackle shop owners in luxury.

Secondhand
Excellent method of obtaining a rod as you can often pick up a deluxe rod hardly used from someone who has just retired.

Kit-Form
A good idea if you are handy and have lots of time and don't

mind getting a dose of 'corkitis' from the dust while making it. Sometimes leads to divorce.

Sections

A rod is made of one, two or three pieces. You can improve on these by running it over with a car, or closing a window or boot on it, thus converting it into what is called multi-piece. The material for construction can be cane, fibre glass, carbon fibre (graphite) or a mixture of glass and carbon. By the way, carbon makes the best lightning conductor. It is also wonderful at transferring electricity from overhead cables and giving you electrical therapy.

Ferrules

These come in male and female form and give the most pleasure when they are a tight fit and do not rotate. If you have problems in getting the male section inserted, use a greasy rag or Brylcreem from your hair. This makes the male section easy to get in. Incidentally if the male and female ferrule get stuck, they cannot be separated by throwing a bucket of water over them. Much easier in the first place to ensure that the female does not get bunged up (different to banged up) than having to use your car and tow-rope to pull the male and female apart.

There are various ways of pulling ferrules apart – brute force, gently twisting to music or crouching down and gripping the rod behind your knees. With this method you use your legs as levers. Not to be recommended if you wear a truss.

The Grip

Generally made from cork and should have a nice feel. Plastic is available but has the disadvantage, unlike cork, that you cannot use it to blacken your face for night fishing.

The Butt

The holding end of the rod, is often given to the fish. Gillies often say 'give it the butt' or 'give it more butt' which means stick it up the fish.

Butt Cap

Can be made of various materials and used to prevent the rod taking out your appendix or castrating you, depending on your stance and style of holding the rod. Butt caps are frequently suitable for screwing and if not checked every time you put your rod up, can get lost. (Not to be confused with Dutch Cap which can have a similar appearance to the Butt Cap).

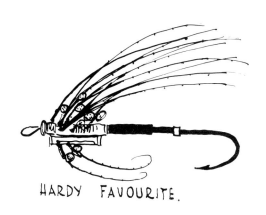

HARDY FAVOURITE.

An angler named Angus McBrae
His rods on the ground he did lay
Along came a cow
Who thought it a wow
And danced. It was Friday the 13th of May

Be careful what you lay on the ground.

Look up as well as down when carrying a rod, especially on strange or new fishing

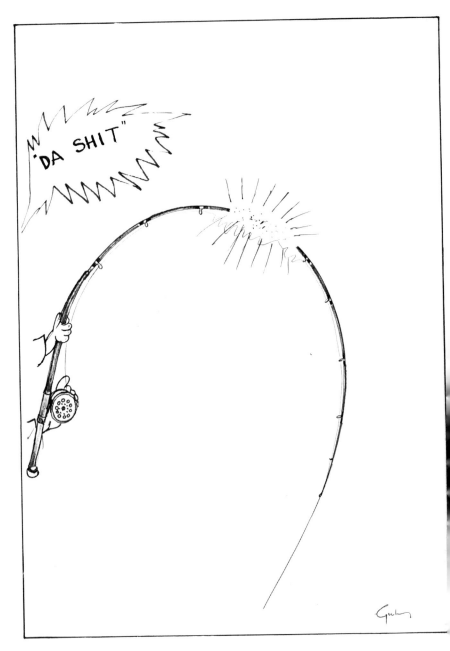

Check your insurance policy to see if fishing tackle is covered. Don't jerk carbon rods

Don't go mad and buy the tackle shop when first taking up fishing. The madness comes naturally very quickly

The right reel for the type of fishing is essential

THE REEL

 T is interesting to look at a dictionary definition of a reel:
'A whirl, be dizzy, swim, sway, stagger, run unsteadily, shaken physically or mentally, rock from side to side, swing violently'.
This describes the average angler going about his day's fishing.

As seen in early paintings, it was the Chinese who were the first to invent the reel. They were used as *takeaways* for fish.

In the Western world the first reels were called winches, derived from the word wenches who frequently wound you up.

The reel, as we know it today, was developed from the early nineteenth century and can still be seen on the river banks of auction rooms where they command huge prices – up to £5,000. This information should not be passed on to skin divers who seek wrecks as they could soon change to river-diving for lost reels and come into contact with wet suited poachers.

The reel is an essential piece of fishing tackle and is made in various materials (see typical specification) and in different sizes. It is also a highland dance which is exhausting and leaves you knackered, which is how a fish should feel, played on a good reel with smooth action, good check and braking system. Sometimes called the 'drag' (this is not to be confused with the way some anglers dress at the water).

The reel should be frequently serviced and given an oil check. A good guide for this is every 6000 fish or every three years.

You can even get reels micro-computerised and simply programmed. The reel's visual display indicates the length of your cast, speed of retrieve and bleeps every second as the cast descends and once for every ten feet of line retrieved, but it takes all the fun out of fishing!

New models, we are told, will be suitable for connecting to T.V. dishes so visual display can give you blue movies when the fish are off the take, and football results. This will enable you on a Saturday to check your pools at the waterside. If you get eight draws you could tell your boss to stick his job and stay on fishing for another week or even buy the water and never go home.

Typical Reel Specification

Frame constructed in light-weight cast iron, with easily chipped enamel finish, reel foot pre-formed to take non-slip foot powder, counterbalanced to prevent the angler falling in when casting. Converts easily from right hand wind to right hand wind.

Quick release spools (Kodak 400 ASA gives best results). Ball bearing mounts that can also be used by tired anglers.

The brake is scientifically calibrated at Harwell and built to British Standards, as was the *Titanic*.

GROUSE and CLARET

The Cure

How do you stop a Scottish boating angler being sea sick on a choppy salmon loch?

Get him to hold a 50p piece in his teeth.

You should be so lucky

Angler out salmon fishing bent down to gaff a salmon when the salmon suddenly twisted and bit off his hand. The angler was rushed to hospital for a transplant.

Unfortunately the only hand available for the transplant was that of his mistress who had died the week before, leaving her body for transplant.

Six weeks later the surgeon asked the angler how his hand was doing.

'Great,' said the angler, 'I can shoot, fish, play tennis and golf, the only problem is when I go for a run-off the hand won't let go.'

Fishy Story

Geordie and Bill at the fishing:

Bill	'I hear you got married yesterday?'
Geordie	'Aye'.
Bill	'Is she good looking?'
Geordie	'No.'
Bill	'Why did you marry her?'
Geordie	'She's got worms.'

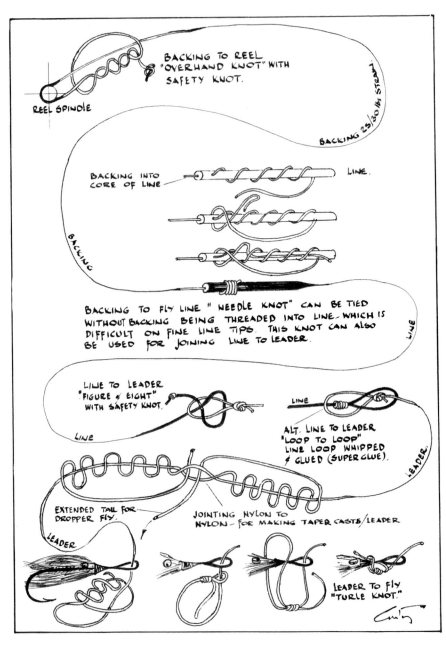

All you need to know in knots from reel to fly

THE LINE

 OMETHING fishermen shoot and without one it is difficult to land a fish (or a wench).

The line should be attached to ample reel backing (not a step in dancing) with a needle knot – so called because forming it gives you the needle and after ten attempts at joining the line to the backing, you end up using super glue, which gives you permanent attachment to the reel, line and backing.

Many years of research, development and testing have gone into the manufacture of fishing lines. However, no one has developed one that does not snag-up in trees or get round boat oars.

The choice of line depends on the water you are fishing, height of water, colour of water, current speed, temperature of water, and air temperature. It can be floating, slow sink, fast sink, neutral sink, sink tip, double tapered, single tapered weight forward. All of these are easily mastered by the novice angler, provided he has a Degree in Line Technology.

Modern fishing lines are easily maintained (if you have a service and anti-cracking contract). They have a long life unless trodden on with wader studs. They should not be used as car tow-ropes or a clothes line in the close season. And they must not get sunburned, frosted or dog-bitten.

The line should always be in balance with the rod. The rod manufacturers indicate the recommended line size with an AFTM number.

The AFTM system uses capital letters.

DT: Double tapered.

WF: Weight forward (forward tapered).

F: Floating.

S: Sinking.

FS: Floaters with sink tip.

ST: Shooting taper or shooting head.

Line sizes are numbered 3 to 12.

A typical salmon rod of 15 to 16 foot, which is a good general purpose rod, would be marked AFTM 11 and a suitable line for greased line fishing would be a DT11F (Double Taper No. 11 Floater), the reel backing should be rot-proof with a strength of 25-30 lbs. 100-150 yards depending on what the reel will contain.

New types of line are coming on the market all the time, which make lift off and casting easier. They are non-cracking, non-stretch or low-stretch, drift-slower, better-striking, easier-bite-detection, more control-power, unaffected by ultra violet light, low co-efficient of friction, high energy casting, automatic-fish-catcher and detector – or so they say!

STEPHENSON

> *An angler who fished doon the Tyne*
> *And cast with a floating greased line*
> *'Why there's nothing,' he sighed*
> *But the gillie replied*
> *'There's more chance doon a flooded coal mine.'*

Manoeuvring the fly on a greased line (floating) requires concentration.
Avoid the fly dragging. Get an even travel of the fly. Air/water temperature is
fairly critical (water temperature high forties F°)

Learn to read the water above and below

Don't learn to cast in à boat – check your insurance policy for rods, boats, dogs, gillie and self

Progress in the Art of Fishing
Yesterday I fished for eight hours and caught nothing, today I fished for six hours and caught nothing – am I improving?

At the Worms
Fishing Grandfather digging worms, watched by his six year old grandson.

'Jimmy I will give you a £1 if you can get one of those worms back down the hole.'

Jimmy, as fast as lightning into the house, comes out with mother's hair spray, sprays the worm, the worm goes rigid, down the hole it goes. Next morning at breakfast Grandfather hands Jimmy a £1 note.

Jimmy says: 'But you paid me last night, Grandad.'

'I know,' says Grandfather, 'that's from your Grandmother.'

Bed & Breakfast
Geordie and Bill fishing miles from home, missed the last bus and had to stay with a widow lady in a bed and breakfast. Some weeks later Geordie met Bill.

Geordie 'Do you mind that time we had to stay with that widow after the fishing?'

Bill 'Yes.'

Geordie 'Did you get up during the night and get into her bed and satisfy her?'

Bill 'Yes.'

Geordie 'Did you give her my name and address?'

Bill 'Yes.'

Geordie 'I'm glad about that. She's left me all her money.'

Notice at the Fishing in Ireland
This car park
subject to river flooding.
When this notice is covered
do not park your car.

Watch your eyes retrieving flies from trees – pull line not rod

A few pounds saved on tackle is often unwise. Buy the best even if it means waiting. The best, properly treated will last for years

THE LEADER
(Sometimes called The Cast)

HIS is a complete misnomer, because usually it does not go anywhere and certainly not in the direction intended.

The leader consists of a length of nylon of the correct strength for the size of the fish you hope to catch but never do. It is used for joining the fly, lure or bait to the line by a mysterious system called knots.

The knots have names like double overhand, turle, or grinner. The most frequently used is the single or double blood knot. This was not its original name but the printer had run short of the letter Y.

Nylon is bought in various breaking strains and thicknesses. The diameter related to strength, has been decreasing over the past few years, so much so that eventually the fish will not be able to see it – or the fisherman to see to knot it.

A tapered leader fishes much better than a straight leader (nothing to do with party politics) and is easily made at the river by a system of bloody knots.

The leader, before being sent out, should be about two thirds the length of the rod and given a strict talking to about tangling, fraternising, associating with bushes, trees, banks, stones and passing vehicles and getting sunburned.

Keep checking the leader for wind knots and if the leader persists in this filthy habit, try dosing with salts or indigestion tablets.

NOTE: The leader can make the fish gut-shy by being too thick. Heavy nylon with small flies makes the leader work-shy and this affects the action of the fly. (See Union Rule Book).

Lick the nylon before pulling tight the knot. This generates less friction and heat and a severed tongue.

Never use old nylon. Sell it to your best friend.

In very windy conditions shorten the leader (an axe is quite handy). This helps a little but does not prevent the disease called 'earpenetration' which can only be cured by packing up and going to the pub.

Burn or cut into small pieces all surplus nylon.

Braided leaders are now available in a large range of tapers, strengths and lengths. These are knotless and easily attached to the fishing line and tippet connections. They reduce tangling and wind knots – ideal for the novice – but will substantially increase your overdraft.

There was an angler, a foolish young fellow
Whose complexion turned a very bright yellow
His lunch he did lay
In the heat of the day
And ended up with a case of salmonella

GENERAL
PRACTITIONER.

Fish are like men, neither would get into trouble if they kept their mouths shut

There once was an old salmon named Bing
Who grew an amazing big thing
But the hens on the redds
As he swam in their beds
Were delighted and spawned with a zing

Red hens should be allowed to occupy redd beds

Don't take your work to the waterside. You don't have to get your finger in up to the elbow. Old forceps are ideal

Dreaded Midge

An angler returning from Scottish fishing holiday.
'Did you fish with flies?'
'Hell yes, I fished with them, ate with them, swallowed them and slept with them.

Careful Drinkers

A fisherman fishing the Dee called at a pub in Aberdeen, asked for a pint of beer, gave a £1 note – and received 98p change.
   'Excuse me you have only charged me 2p for that pint of beer.'
   'That's right,' replied the barman, 'it's the 50th anniversary of the pub and we are charging the drinks at the prices 50 years ago.'
   'Then why are those people waiting outside?'
   'Oh they're waiting for the Happy Hour to start'!

Scottish Angler's Lament

Sometimes ower early, sometimes ower late.
Sometimes nae wauter, sometimes in a spate.
Sometimes ower dirty, sometimes ower clear.
Something always wrang when I'm fishing here.

Left Right or Centre

Every time Geordie went boat fishing with Bill whichever side of the boat he chose to fish from he caught fish.
   One day Bill said, 'Geordie, how is it that every time we go fishing you choose the best side to fish. How do you know which side of the boat the fish are going to be?'
   'Well,' said Geordie, 'it's easy. If I wake up in the morning and the wife is lying on her left, I fish the left side of the boat. If she's on her right side I fish from the right side of the boat.'
   'That's all very well,' said Bill, 'but what if she's on her back?'
   'Then you won't be seeing me at the fishing till much later.'

HOOKS

 NLY buy the best, for only the best will stay in your ear or hand that little bit longer and won't let you down when you eventually hook a salmon.

The size is a slight problem in that not all manufacturers conform to a standard scale.

The cross section of the hook is known as the gauge and described by an X System . . . 2X 3X.

The smaller the number, the bigger the hook. Some hooks are bronze, others have black finish and the basic types for salmon are as follows:–

Trebles: No. 4, 6, 8, 10: No. 6 and 8 being the most popular size for tube flies, Devons, tubes and spoons.

Outbend Trebles: No. 6, 8, 10, 12, very good hooking, hold well.

Double Salmon: 2/0 to 12.

Double Low Water: 2 to 12.

Some manufacturers have other sizes.

Singles: No. 5/0 to No. 12.

Single low water: No. 1 to No. 12.

There are many other variations, but these will cover you for most aspects of salmon fishing and all are equal for the art of acupuncture.

Number 6 and number 8 trebles are the most popular general sizes with number 10 and 12 for low water or greased line (floating line) fishing.

Finally, never use a hook that is rusty; it will cut through nylon like butter and unless your tetanus injections are up to date you may end up with a bad dose of lockjaw. You certainly won't end up with a fish on the bank.

Try to forget work and relax at the fishing. Fishing is a great stress reliever, until you lose a fish

FISHING FLIES OR FLEES

 OBODY quite knows why a salmon takes a fly but with so many hundreds of patterns tied on single, double or treble hooks, flying in and out of the water no wonder a salmon eventually gets round to taking one. But if salmon are not on the take, go down in fly size or go down to the pub.

Keep checking the barb on the hook especially after bouncing the fly off rocks behind you. When fishing a fly tied on double or treble hooks make sure that it has not turned on the leader and given him a 'kick in the bends'.

Many fishing flies are now tied in Africa, using monkey hair, lion hair, zebra hair and deer hair. In fact many fishers could open their fly boxes to the public and charge an entry fee just like a safari park.

Learn to tie your own flies. There is no greater thrill than catching a fish on your fly. It also saves you appearing in court for indecent exposure. The best fly to select is one you have confidence in and which has caught fish. This, however, requires that you catch a fish in the first place. This is called the *parr and egg* syndrome.

The following is a good starter collection in two or three sizes:

Stoat's Tail	*Monro*	*Jock Scott*
Hairy Mary	*Garry*	*Red Shrimp*
Silver Doctor	*Black Shrimp*	

Tube flies come in sizes from half inch to three inch. They can be dressed on heavy, medium or light-weight tubes. For greased line fishing they are often dressed on PVC or nylon tubes. This is a very easy fly to dress yourself. The bodies, undressed and lined, can be obtained from any good tackle shop.

Be very careful when fishing large tube flies, especially in windy conditions. They hurt like hell if they hit you in the middle of the back from a faulty cast. Always wear a hat that gives protection to ears as well as the head.

A Waddington is a very popular fly and is basically a tube fly dressed on wire with a permanently attached treble. The various items for dressing this fly are available from any good tackle shop. A length of heavy nylon wrapped round the bends of the treble and tied into the body keeps the treble in line with the body.

Flies are always being invented, the latest now extends into the pharmaceutical domain, with a fly developed by the Americans. This has a hollow head to take Alka Seltzer in powder form. When the fly is pulled through the water it emits a string of tiny bubbles (can also be stuck on the tongue and sucked to clear hangovers).

BUTCHER.

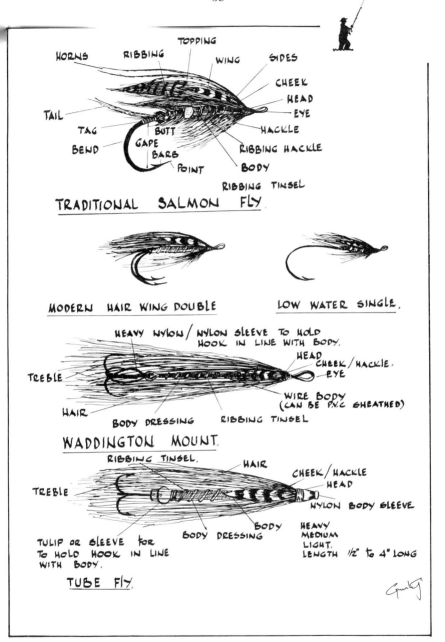

HORNS
RIBBING
TOPPING
WING
SIDES
CHEEK
HEAD
EYE
HACKLE
TAIL
TAG
BUTT
GAPE
BARB
POINT
BEND
RIBBING HACKLE
BODY
RIBBING TINSEL

TRADITIONAL SALMON FLY.

MODERN HAIR WING DOUBLE

LOW WATER SINGLE.

HEAVY NYLON / NYLON SLEEVE TO HOLD
HOOK IN LINE WITH BODY.
HEAD
CHEEK / HACKLE.
EYE
TREBLE
HAIR
BODY DRESSING
RIBBING TINSEL
WIRE BODY
(CAN BE P.V.C SHEATHED)

WADDINGTON MOUNT.

RIBBING TINSEL.
HAIR
CHEEK / HACKLE
HEAD
TREBLE
NYLON BODY SLEEVE
BODY
BODY DRESSING
HEAVY
MEDIUM
LIGHT.
LENGTH 1/2" to 4" LONG
TULIP OR SLEEVE for
To HOLD HOOK IN LINE
WITH BODY.

TUBE FLY.

There are hundreds of variations and patterns of salmon flies many designed
and dressed to catch the angler, not the fish

Check the water conditions before making a long journey

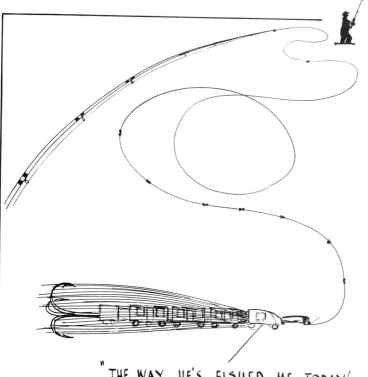

" THE WAY HE'S FISHED ME TODAY!
I WOULD HAVE HAD A BETTER
CHANCE OF A FISH ON THE
PICCADILLY LINE "

TUBE FLY	BODY	RIBBING	WING	HACKLE/CHECK
Comet	Red Silk Floss	Flat Silver Tinsel	Layered Black/Red Yellow Bucktail	Jungle Cock optional
Hairy Mary	Black Silk Floss	Oval Gold Tinsel	Red/Brown Squirrel	Blue Hackle Squirrel
Blue Charm	Black Silk Floss	Oval Silver Tinsel	Grey Squirrel Tail or Badger	Blue Hackle Squirrel
Silver Wilkinson	Red Silk Floss	Flat Broad Tinsel	Magenta Bucktail	Teal Body Feathers and Jungle Cock
Garry	Red Silk Floss	Flat Narrow Silver Tinsel	Mixed Red and Yellow Bucktail	Jungle Cock optional

There once was an angler called 'Mary'
Attractive, but ever so 'Hairy'
Our Willie did see
While tying the flee
And changed its name from the 'Black Fairy'

Tying flies from a model can give pulling results

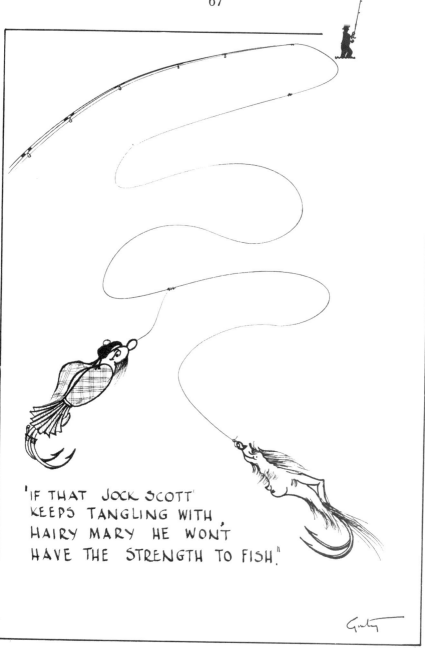

Fishing the dropper can give problems both in the water and in the landing net

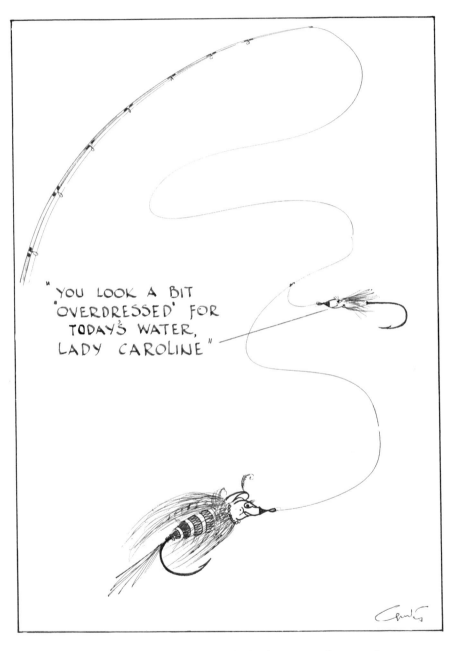

Choosing the size and dressing of a fly for the water, only comes from experience, or the use of a crystal ball

A lot of flies are tied to catch anglers, not fish. You do however, get good –
taking flies

Gillies would be well advised to wear a cricket box

THE ART OF CASTING

HE art of projecting a lure or fly on a line, on to or into the water (or bank) without scaring the living daylights out of the fish. There are various methods of casting a fly line, the simplest being the faulty cast. This is easily carried out by the novice angler and the easiest way to improve this is to have someone take a video of you casting, or stand in front of a mirror. This will convince you to have casting lessons from a professional or get your hair cut.

Because the art of casting is all in the timing, it is therefore important to have a reliable waterproof watch, as we are frequently told not to go further back than the one o'clock position. (For further information on positions see *Kama Sutra*).

The advantage of a waterproof watch is that it comes to no harm when you fall in the river while practising.

CASTING METHODS

Overhead
Essential if you want to catch everything in your rear and sometimes including your ears.

Underhand
It's a bit like insider dealing and used by people in the financial world.

Roll Cast
Best when using egg and cress for bait.

Single Spey

This is the most useful when you cannot cast overhead and ensures that the line and fly land perfectly round your head and the fly is implanted in your right or left ear, depending which shoulder you are casting off (not to be confused with knitting terminology although sometimes the line does end up like wool pulled out of a jumper).

Double Spey

This is not a Scottish reel or dance, although when you see some anglers attempting this cast you would think it was. It is basically the same as the Single Spey and can be fished with two flies ensuring you get one in the right and one in the left ear.

Mending the Line

This is done after the cast has just landed on to the water and prevents a belly being formed in the line by the river current. The line is best mended by super glue and the belly by less drinking.

The False Cast

This is done to scare the fish and consists of lifting the line out of the water, casting at half the angle downstream that you intended, lifting off again and correcting the next cast, in all a very tiring way of fishing.

The distance you cast is dependent on the water being fished. It is very rare that you need to cast more than 25-30 yards. In fact very few individuals can cast well at this distance.

When casting with a fast-sink line and a tube fly or Waddington, retrieve line, lift the remaining line out of the water till you can see the line/leader knot, then proceed to cast, shooting the retrieved line. Failure to do this could result in an end to the day's fishing and an insurance claim for a new rod.

Rods do break but very rarely if fished properly.

However, the most likely chance of breaking a rod is not when casting but in sudden jerking of the rod when hanked on the bottom or up a tree.

GREEN HIGHLANDER.

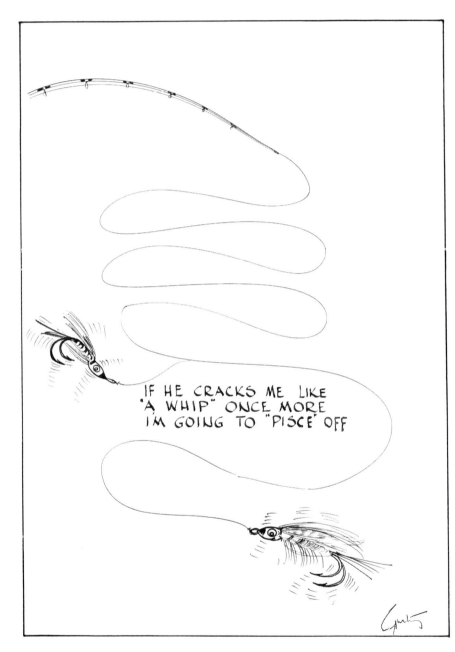

Cracking off flies is an expensive hobby

'Well scholar, you must endure worse luck sometime, or you will never make a good angler.' (*Compleat Angler*, Izaak Walton, 1653)

You cannot always get what you want locally

HOOKING PLAYING AND LANDING THE FISH

HE amount of literature and advice written on the subject of hooking or striking a fish could fill a dust-bin, and should.

For me, the golden rule is to let the fish take from the reel. A lot of people will disagree with this and suggest having slack line between the reel and the line-holding hand. They are entitled to their opinion.

Let the fish hook itself, then it can blame nobody but itself. Modern reels have superb actions which allow the tension to be set for a smooth take off from the reel when the fish takes.

Hooking comes with experience. The highlight of angling for salmon is the experience and delight of *rising* and hooking a salmon. (Hen fish are known as hookers.)

Having let the fish hook itself, preferably in the mouth, you then have to get it into your car boot. This is called playing the fish. Unfortunately, it is often the case that the fish does not understand the rules of the game and plays you. It is far better and safer on the nervous system if a fish comes off in the first few seconds of playing as there is nothing more frustrating than losing a fish after ten minutes. If you do lose the fish you will never know what size it was except when telling fellow anglers about it and that it was the biggest you have ever hooked.

The best way to play a fish, if wading, is to get out of the water and on to the river bank as soon as possible, but not with so much haste that you fall, arse over tit on rocks at your rear.

Keep a tight line from the hooking to the landing and try to be opposite the fish all the time. This is not always easy, as hooked fish often want to take off and to get opposite or in touch with the fish requires a No. 10 bus. Don't give the fish too much line. If it takes you down to your backing pray like hell that the line-backing knot you last tested five years ago will hold.

If possible never let a large belly form in the line between rod and fish called *drowning the line*. It does not matter if you get drowned, but the drowning is a punishable offence, as the penalty is generally a lost fish.

The strain you put on the fish comes from experience and should be proportionate to the strength of the leader and gauge of the hook.

Depending on the size, an average time for landing a fish is 5-10 minutes, although if you get into a really large fish, and depending on the river conditions, this could extend to 40-60 minutes or longer if you are late home.

You can often *walk a fish up*. This means that if a fish is making its way down stream to rapids or the pool below you, you hang on like hell hoping the cast or knot will not break or the fish says, 'Stuff this for a lark', and starts making its way back to you. You can then take control of the fish and say to your fellow anglers 'Yes, I walked him up and then beached him.'

There are numerous ways of getting the fish on to the bank. First wait till the fish is played out (knackered). This is easily recognised as the fish turns on its side and shows you its white bum and then makes several mad efforts to get off.

The Landing Net

This is always assuming that you have a net handy. Generally you are so browned off carrying it about that you leave it lying on the bank about two miles away.

Never try to land a salmon in a small net. It won't like it. A big net with a thick handled telescopic extension is ideal. It is a delight to watch an experienced gillie as he nets a fish, this also allows you to start breathing again if it's your fish.

Many anglers make a right mess of netting a salmon by trying to dig it out of the river. (Digging should be confined to worms).

The net should be submerged, the mesh being held down by a large pebble, the fish should be steered head down over the net, the net should then be closed like a purse with the rim of the net just out of the water and then moved gently back to the bank.

The angler should release the line tension off the fly as soon as the net closes around the fish. This prevents the fly from turning into a missile and giving you a one-eyed gillie or brother fisherman.

Lift the net and fish, well up the bank – about half a mile if you don't want the fish to leap back into the water.

Watching many anglers trying to net a fish themselves, would make a classic film worthy of Charlie Chaplin.

To kill the fish, leave it in the net, then hit it on the head with a *priest*, so called because you administer the last rites. This is why there is no fishing in Scotland on Sunday, because, as on the river bank, the *priest* is never available.

The Gaff

The least said about this the better. On some rivers it is not allowed at all and on others only at certain times of the season. It would be better if the times of no gaffing were from December to December.

The Tailer

The tailer is an ingenious piece of tackle consisting of a tubular handle from which a wire rabbit-type snare extends for a noose, the other end of the handle has a carrying loop.

The theory is that while you are playing the fish you remove the tailer, which you carry round your neck and shoulder by extending the wire-loop-noose passing over your hat and under your armpit, so it acts like a tourniquet.

Removing the tailer from your neck whilst holding on to the rod and fish, you always manage to knock your hat into the water (see sections on dog training). You then loop the holding cord at the handle, round your wrist (provided the fish is still on) and then proceed to bring the fish to a depth of water that will allow you to slip the rabbit snare around its tail and pull like hell allowing the holding ring of the snare to slip round the bow of the snare. The reason for looping the holding cord around your wrist, is that if the fish takes off, it takes you with it.

The tailer is very useful on rocky and steep banks or for big fish. Again it requires great experience to use correctly. You very rarely see a gillie using one.

Beaching

This is the best solution or method of landing a fish, provided you can find a dry dock harbour or a piece of river bank with a gentle slope.

You simply play the fish till it shows signs of being tired or fed up, reel in as far as possible then walk backwards if possible, watching behind you and at the same time directing the fish to the place of beaching. You are almost certain to trip over a branch or boulder. Once the fish is on to semi-dry land it tends to lie quite still and is reasonably easy to hand-tail.

Fish can be hand-tailed in deeper water, but this requires courage and a certain amount of experience.

Hand-tailing a sea trout is extremely difficult, your grip can slip off due to lack of wrist to grip.

FRUIT FLY.

Find out the going rate (tip) for the water, unless stipulated in lease

Fishing is a bit of a gamble. Gambling at the water is dangerous. Fish caught in scissors, confusing when they are in his hand

Don't believe all fishing stories, especially about good salmon fishing at £1 a day per rod. The best is very expensive

Salmon rarely take on rising water

The only time a fisherman tells the truth is when he calls another fisherman a liar

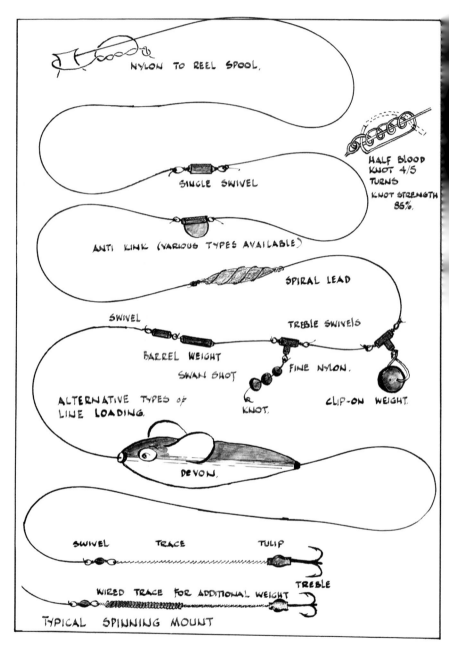

NYLON TO REEL SPOOL.

HALF BLOOD KNOT 4/5 TURNS

KNOT STRENGTH 85%.

SINGLE SWIVEL

ANTI KINK (VARIOUS TYPES AVAILABLE)

SPIRAL LEAD

SWIVEL

TREBLE SWIVELS

BARREL WEIGHT

SWAN SHOT

FINE NYLON.

ALTERNATIVE TYPES OF LINE LOADING.

KNOT.

CLIP-ON WEIGHT.

DEVON.

SWIVEL   TRACE   TULIP

TREBLE

WIRED TRACE FOR ADDITIONAL WEIGHT

TYPICAL SPINNING MOUNT

Avoid making your line look like a Christmas decoration

SPINNING WITH BAITS AND LURES

The Devon

O named because it is the cream of baits for spinning. They can be purchased in all colours, and made of metal, metal and wood or plastic. They are all designed with fins that break off and ensure constant visits to the tackle shop. (If they suffer from jaundice they are called *Yellow Bellies*). Fins can be replaced with tags from beer cans, which is a good excuse for opening cans of beer at the river and why you see so many discarded beer cans on the bank.

Devons are sometimes called Minnows when fished upstream and dragged through the pools and rocks at a hell of a rate. This is called upstream minnow and frequently catches 'rock salmon'. The Devon/ Minnow is mounted on a treble hook system called a trace which can be weighted to suit river conditions.

Toby Type

This is a flat piece of metal shaped like a fish with a slight twist, this causes the bait to jink and come out of the fish's mouth. The treble hook at the tail of the bait is attached with a single split ring. Many anglers fit two split rings to give the hooked fish less leverage. The first ring is called the engagement ring and the second the marriage and costs nearly as much.

So many metal baits have been lost or hanked up on river bottoms that if they were all recovered and sent for scrap it would close down five major steelworks throughout the world.

The Toby-type comes in many colours; copper, bronze, gold,

black and silver. For little extra cost your local jeweller can give an additional flash to the bait by mounting diamonds, rubies or emeralds.

To keep the treble hook and split rings more in line with the bait, anglers sometimes tape them up or use heavy nylon and tape. Wire can also be used to make a flying mount (not to be confused with window cleaners and milkmen who get paid in kind in absence of angling husbands).

Mepps Type
This bait is the original French spinner and is sometimes dressed with feathers and hair to make it look like a can-can dancer. The Mepp can be fitted with rotating blades that emit vibrating sounds which call the fish from far and wide. In fact you can be fishing for salmon in a river in Scotland and catch a fish from a Spanish river. Works better than 'Spanish fly'.

Spoon Type
This is a cross between a Mepp and a Toby. Rich anglers have them engraved with their family crest or initials, which makes them highly sought after by collectors of fishing tackle.

Rapola
This is one of the most expensive lures you can buy. Very rarely used in Scotland. It is multi-coloured and made from wood, metal or plastic with a flat disc stuffed up the nose of the bait, which makes it dart about and fish very deep; so deep that when fished in the U.K., anglers frequently end up playing a fish in Australia.

The list of lures is endless but the Americans corner the market for names such as Deepwee, Bang-O-Luke, (for fishing with girlfriend) Chatter B, Hula Popper, Sputterbuzz, Rattle Spin, Whopper Stopper, Ba You Boogies, Deep Hog, Deep Pig, Wally Driver, Road Runner, Crappie Jigs, Crappie Queen,

Lindy, Fuzz-E-Grub, Chatter Box, Little George, Lazy Ike, Wiggler, Reeker, Walleye Gitters, Jigheads. And if you don't believe me just read an American tackle catalogue.

Note: Any young anglers wanting to start a pop group need look no further than these baits for a band name.

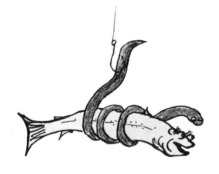

STRANGLER (WORM FLY)

Don't fish baits too fast. Let the current carry the bait round. Only fast wind on upstream-minnow

Always stretch new nylon and use good quality swivels and anti-kink devices

Advice from the Pulpit

An enthusiastic but boring angling vicar decided on Sunday to give a sermon on abstention from drink which went on at great length and ended with a demonstration. He took two glasses and filled one with water and the other with gin. Taking hold of a worm he dropped it into the glass containing the gin, the worm immediately dropped to the bottom of the glass dead. He then took another worm and dropped it into the glass containing the water and the worm swam happily around. 'What is the moral of this demonstration?' asked the vicar of his congregation.

'If you've got worms drink gin,' replied the fed-up choir boy.

End of the Week

Doc Fisherfax   'Do you know Willie that one salmon we caught this week has cost me £1000.'

Willie   'Then it's a good job ye didnae catch two.'

Sporting Comparisons

A golfer has an enormous advantage over a fisherman – he doesn't have to produce anything to prove his story.

Gale on a Salmon Loch

Owner   'Come in number 99, it's too dangerous.'
No response.
Owner   'Come in, it's too choppy.'
No response.
Owner   'Come in, it's too windy.'
No response.
Owner   'Are you alright number 66?'

"HE MUST BE RICH HE USES REAL OTTERS."

Always use an otter when hanked up. Don't jerk rods. A bottle or piece of branch tied with a loop of nylon round the line makes a bank-side otter

The lawn is the best location on a warm night. A red light is best, you also get funny visitors

NATURAL BAITS

FFECTIONATELY called snakes by salmon fishers, worms have been used for centuries. Mounted on bent pins and safety pins it is the apprenticeship bait for young anglers.

A ten year apprenticeship is required before you become expert at this form of fishing. Constant physiotherapy treatment is required for a complaint called wormitis, caused by digging or stooping down to collect the bait. The best worms for salmon fishing are lobworms, so named because you lob them into the water. They are sometimes called night crawlers because of the action of anglers seeking them by torch at night; not to be confused with kerb crawlers who have the same actions.

Worms can be collected either by using a vibrating stake driven twelve inches into the ground (worms come out of the ground shaking their heads) or watering the ground with soapy water (worms come up out of the ground squeaky clean).

Americans use an Electro Worm Getter 110 volt prodding stick (operates like the electric chair).

Worms are best kept in a rust proof container filled with wet newspaper and moss. This scours (toughens) them in about four days. The best newspaper to use is the Sunday Times; this will make them appeal to a better class of salmon. If you store then in a Fortnum and Mason biscuit tin, it is called up-market worming. Storage temperature 60 degrees farenheit. Temperatures over 70-75 degrees farenheit is fatal.

Fish the worm by keeping in touch and allowing the line out on the take before striking (BT and union at present working on this).

Shrimps and Prawns

These are deadly when fishing for salmon and are banned on many rivers. If arranged in the form of a cocktail they can be used as a starter before using other baits.

A prawn fished through a salmon pool will frequently excite fish so much that they start playing with it. It also has the effect of moving the salmon up to the next beat.

Shrimp and prawn can be fished from a fly or spinning rod, with the cast weighted to suit the speed and depth of the river.

Sprats

These are small fish caught in the sea. They are silver and gold and should not be the size of kippers.

They are preserved in a solution that is used for keeping dead bodies for medical science – and it certainly smells like it. Goodness knows what the highly sensitive nose of the salmon thinks about them. They are mounted on specially weighted mounts festooned with hooks. The sprat is made to swallow the weight and is then wrapped with copper wire so it looks like the windings of an electrical motor.

It is advisable to carry Brillo pads, soap, scrubbing brush, pummice stone and deodorant to get rid of the smell from your hands after mounting this type of bait. Many an angler gets his mother-in-law to prepare and mount a number of sprats before going fishing – it is a form of revenge. The sprat should be fished like a Toby or Devon, with a very slow wind. This helps get rid of the smell during the first fifty casts. The salmon attacks this type of bait, probably in protest at such an infringement of civil liberties in the river.

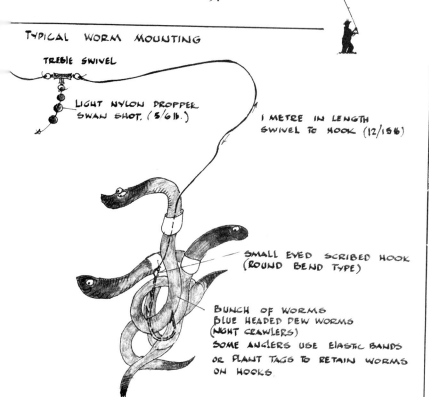

TYPICAL WORM MOUNTING

TREBLE SWIVEL

LIGHT NYLON DROPPER
SWAN SHOT. (5/6 lb.)

1 METRE IN LENGTH
SWIVEL TO HOOK (12/15 lb)

SMALL EYED SCRIBED HOOK
(ROUND BEND TYPE)

BUNCH OF WORMS
BLUE HEADED DEW WORMS
(NIGHT CRAWLERS)
SOME ANGLERS USE ELASTIC BANDS
OR PLANT TAGS TO RETAIN WORMS
ON HOOKS.

RULES for WORMING

1. Keep worms for 4/6 days in well aired box containing newspaper and moss.
2. Do not allow storage temperature to exceed 70°/75°F.
3. Use good quality scribed hooks.
4. Don't be mean with worms. Mount large bunch. Keep changing.
5. Use swivel with weights – experiment with weights to get worms to trundle down pool in an arc, very slowly.
6. Cast up-stream.
7. Keep in touch with worms. Hold Line. Brake off reel.
8. Try to avoid worms snagging on bottom. Keep rod tip up.
9. Fish down pool or lie slowly and be systematic – moving down river in small steps, covering the whole lie. Salmon smell worms.
10. Eels and small trout often a problem.
11. Learn the difference between eel, trout and salmon takes.
12. Salmon tend to move with worms when taking – allow 2/3 metres of line to run off reel before striking.
13. Experience is necessary. To watch an expert worming is an education and well worth while.

Some anglers use two hooks in tandem. Don't fish too fine a cast. 12/15 lb main line, 5/6 lb dropper/weights.

Jack and Jill went up the hill
He thought to do some fishing
But Jill lay down
And, 'For half a crown
I'll show you what you're missing'

Always ensure that you have money with you when you go fishing for tips and
other unforeseen items

Fish worms slowly – keep in touch by holding the line with brake off – allow fish to take line before striking. Salmon smell worms

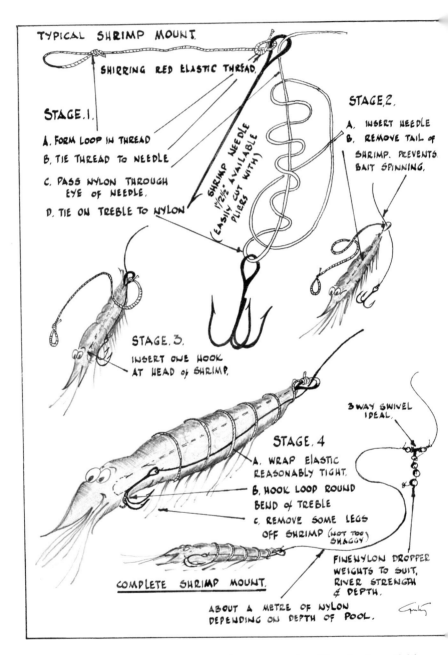

TYPICAL SHRIMP MOUNT.

SHIRRING RED ELASTIC THREAD.

STAGE.1.

A. FORM LOOP IN THREAD

B. TIE THREAD TO NEEDLE

C. PASS NYLON THROUGH
   EYE OF NEEDLE.

D. TIE ON TREBLE TO NYLON

SHRIMP NEEDLE
1"/2½" AVAILABLE
(EASILY CUT WITH)
PLIERS

STAGE.2.

A. INSERT NEEDLE

B. REMOVE TAIL OF
   SHRIMP. PREVENTS
   BAIT SPINNING.

STAGE.3.

INSERT ONE HOOK
AT HEAD OF SHRIMP.

STAGE.4

A. WRAP ELASTIC
   REASONABLY TIGHT.

B. HOOK LOOP ROUND
   BEND OF TREBLE

C. REMOVE SOME LEGS
   OFF SHRIMP (NOT TOO SHAGGY)

3 WAY SWIVEL
IDEAL.

FINENYLON DROPPER
WEIGHTS TO SUIT,
RIVER STRENGTH
& DEPTH.

COMPLETE SHRIMP MOUNT.

ABOUT A METRE OF NYLON
DEPENDING ON DEPTH OF POOL.

There are numerous variations on shrimp mounting. If no elastic available, use loops of nylon at the head and the tail of the shrimp

Make sure you have a good supply of matched traces and minnows

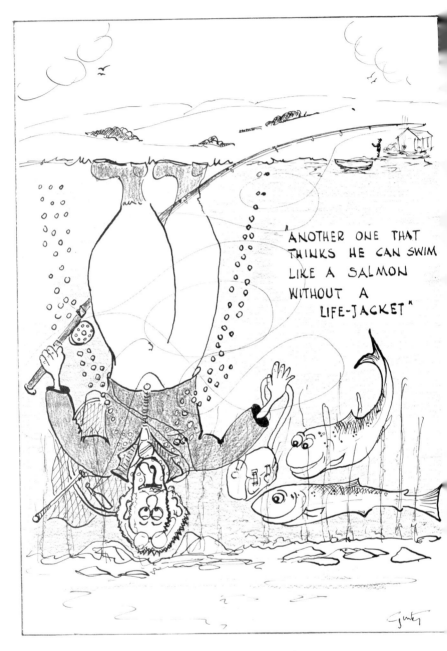

Never wade – without aid

THE ART OF WADING

Thy rod and thy staff and fall-in-kit shall accompany you all the days of your fishing.

F you cannot swim don't attempt to wear chest or belly waders (chest or belly depending on your figure).

Learn to wade in thigh waders before attempting the slow, slow, quick, quick, slow of the belly-wading-dance.

Try waders with two pairs of socks before buying. (Take your own socks – in some tackle shops the socks are unwashed for 40 years).

Buy a repair kit and barbed wire detector (can be bought in one box).

Keep your repair kit in the car or fishing bag (not much good at home if you are in North Alaska and get a leak).

Felt-soled waders are fine in the water. Out of the water, on wet grass, mud, snow and ice, they will put you in competition with Torvill and Dean.

Keep wader studs up to scratch (useful if you get an itchy back).

Always hang up waders after using. (This allows the smell to escape).

Do not dry too quickly near a fire. (Doing this keeps half the population in Taiwan in work).

If you do fall in (you will fall in) waders are difficult to dry. Use a plastic bag (after taking out your sandwiches) on each foot. This, at least, keeps your fall-in-kit socks dry till the next time you fall in. (Having written this it sounds Irish).

Good waders are like gold. By that I mean the seams are like gold seams; they get worked out very quickly. Some pairs you see at the river should be entered for a patch-work quilt competition.

Wading Stick
Select your wading stick with great care. It should be firm and not flex. It must have a good strong cord with reliable attachments, such as a rubber foot for silent wading, (and for silence when praying to catch a fish) depth gauge and sonic finder. It can be purchased with built-in thermometer which is useful for taking the water temperature or diagnosing if you have the flu coming on after falling in.

A good wading stick should be like a truss and give you all the support you need.

Never wade deeper than you feel is comfortable. It is easy wading with the current, but you need a 10 h.p. outboard motor to help you wade back up against the current.

Get to know the water before wading in.

To find leaks in waders:
    Put on gas mask.
    Place head inside waders.
    This will enable you to see even the smallest hole.

It makes good sense to wear some form of life or buoyancy jacket, especially when in new water with a slippy bottom. Talcum powder may help overcome this problem.

Always eat a tin of peas or beans before wearing chest waders in winter (farting acts just like central heating).

THUNDER AND LIGHTNING

Always burn or cut into small pieces nylon before throwing away – unkind to wildlife

Even the smallest of pin pricks can be detected, provided you can endure the smell

With all the pollution changes to the environment this could be a real possibility

He that wades so deep, can make a gillie weep (and maybe his widow)

Always carry a Fall In Kit and a large towel. You may need to give a fellow-angler a rub down

CLOTHES FOR THE FISHING

ATS come in all sorts of shapes and sizes and when worn at the river make the angler look as if he is on his way to a fancy dress party.

The hat must be capable of floating, staying on in a force 10 gale, and give protection from hooks to the back of the neck and ears. Colour, shape and waterproof qualities are minor details.

The size is dictated by the number of flies the hat can accommodate to the square inch.

Gillies are known to wear A.R.P. tin hats, German steel helmets (ideal ear protection) old motor cycle helmets and plastic site hats.

It is not unknown for a gillie fishing with an awful ear-pricking caster, to go home for lunch and come back wearing a dust-bin lid.

Underwear

Warm layers of underwear and longjohns are essential for spring and autumn fishing. Nothing beats wool, preferably after it has been taken off the sheep's back.

Silk underwear can be worn, but it will be treated with suspicion by fellow anglers and will stop them bending down to pick things off the ground or tail fish.

Shirt

Shirts must be loose-fitting and dark in colour. This allows for them to be washed only once in every fishing season.

They should have a good pocket with buttoned flap to get the angler into the habit of putting his car keys somewhere safe. This avoids having to join the AA and RAC, or putting a brick through the car window to get to the ignition where you left them when you locked the car.

Sweaters

Known as jumpers to older anglers; they should be bought two sizes larger than you require. Constant immersion in water shrinks them.

They should never be red as there is enough bull talked at the water without attracting any more.

Towel/Scarf

This stops water dripping down the neck and is ideal for taking drips off the nose before they freeze. It can also be used for wiping tears away after losing a fish. Plus it looks the part.

Old school scarves can also be worn provided the colour suits you and does not clash with green. They also remind you of your youth especially when hooking a mermaid.

Trousers

Any old trousers will do, provided they are not so tight that they strangle your testicles whilst bending to tail, net or beach fish.

The most comfortable trousers are fishing breeches with elastic leg cuffs and reinforced in the crutch to protect your balls when crossing barbed wire fences or taking a blow from a flying toby, yanked up by your constant tugging and jerking, and returning in your direction like a bullet.

Socks

A most important item of clothing. Uncomfortable socks can ruin a day's fishing.

The new anti-smell socks are a boon to the river wild life and fellow anglers travelling home with you in the car.

Remember that well known saying by Izaac Walton:

'When toes are cold the fish don't hold'.

(Izaac Walton – the Jewish stocking maker, not the one that wrote the *Compleat Angler*).

Fall-In-Kit
Duplicate all items of clothing especially in winter.

Special Note: If you see a bra or roll-ons in a fellow fisher's Fall-In-Kit, he could either be a woman, gay – or have been wearing such items since the wife found them in the back of his car.

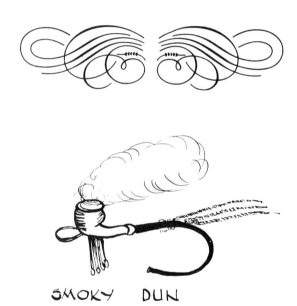

SMOKY DUN

This portrait of willie is an unusual sight
Since that 'Flaps Down' terrible night
He was offered a beer
Which he never did hear
He now has them fastened up tight

Always protect your ear and back of neck when fishing with big flies

Always try your fishing clothes on at home or in the shop

Don't carry unnecessary tackle. It weighs twice as much at the end of a day's fishing

Before purchase, always try on waders with additional socks

Always keep a loo roll in the car – wrapped in cling film

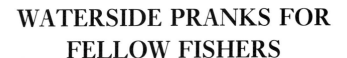

WATERSIDE PRANKS FOR FELLOW FISHERS

LACE a rotten egg in each colleague's wader leg, this always gets the day's fishing off to a good start.

Place a live eel in the bog. This always amuses the ladies in the party and endears them to fishing holidays.

Reverse pawl in fellow angler's reel so the brake does not work. This causes great amusement when he hooks his first fish on a Saturday after a blank week's fishing.

Teach your dog to steal other people's sandwiches.

Put fellow fisher's tin of worms on the hot stove in the fishing hut. This not only cooks them, but the smell in the hut is hilarious.

Teach your dog to pee into fishing friends' Fall-In-Kit. This is guaranteed a laugh especially if they have cause to use their Fall-in-Kit some months after the event.

Wait till your friend has tied on a fly and file off the barb. This again is great fun when he hooks the first fish of the season.

Feed your dog a tin of Heinz Beans and lock in fishing hut as you go off to fish in the morning. The effect on your friends returning to the hut for lunch is breathtaking.

Bring six fishing friends for a week's fishing on a one rod beat. This is much funnier if the water is very low.

Keep dogs under control at the river. Some beats don't allow dogs. – Read 'Country Code for Dogs'.

TAKING YOUR DOG FISHING

IRST of all take your dog to obedience classes so it can fully understand commands like 'Get out of the bloody water!' Train your dog to close gates after you.

Digging holes is natural for dogs, so this could be encouraged, together with retrieving worms. The holes can also be used for burying rubbish so frequently left by anglers who do not have dogs and couldn't care a damn.

Keep your dog on a lead. This ensures that when you are fishing you will trip arse over tit into the river.

Train your dog to retrieve. This is useful when your hat blows or falls into the river, or helping you out when you fall in. Discrete retrieving training is useful when the fishing is surrounded by game birds.

GROCER.

ANGLER'S WEDDING LIST
(Leave Open At All Times)

 TAINLESS steel thermos flasks.

Hand warmers and tights.

Good mitts (finger flaps large size, they shrink).

Tackle box (not too large).

Towel.

Scarves (two).

Bottle Opener and Corkscrew (essential at the water).

Polaroid Glasses (top quality).

Small Pliers (for removing hooks from fingers and ears.

Good Hat or Cap (Caps with flaps).

First Aid Kit (plastic bag or container type).

Insect Repellent and Sun Cream.

Roll of Nylon Sleeve for Packing Fish (will last for years).

Thermal Fish Holding Bag with Liners.

Good Fishing Shirt (with buttoned pocket for car keys).

Set of Heavy Duty Jump Leads (surprising how often used).

Can of WD40 (for releasing last year's reel action).

Box of Strong Elastic Bands (ever useful).

Two rolls of Electricians' Tape (most borrowed item at river).

Good Quality Torch (waterproof).

Fly Tying Vice (good quality).

Scissors (with forceps).

Priest (with arrangement for attaching cord).

Strong Canvas Bag (for Fall-In-Kit).

Wool Longjohns (M. & S. sell super ones).

Rod Carriers (check car for magnetic type and gutters).

Plastic Rod Carrying Tubes (can reduce no claims bonus).

Old and New Fishing Books (check with relations before ordering and purchasing).

Wading Stick (heavy, good hand-grip, non-floating).

Box of Salmon Flies (selection of 2 sizes of the following will guarantee a marriage success). Hairy Mary, Jock Scott, Monro, Stoat's Tail, Garry, Red Shrimp, Black Shrimp, Silver Doctor.

Boot Driers (essential to go with Fall-In-Kit).

Wader Repair Kit (will be used often).

Real Leather Reel Cases (twin and single).

Battery Alarm Clock

Combined Fishing Vest and Life Buoyancy Jacket.

Up Market Presents

:ﺷ—ﻪ: ﻙ.—ﻒ :ﺍ : ﻃ (Range Rover).

:ﺟﻄ ﺀ:. ﺝ. ﺿ ﺀ·—ﺍ ﺽ·ﻱ .ﺍﻝ . (Stretch of River).

ﺝ! ﺀ—ﺍﻝﺝﻝ ﺟﺖ :—ﺏ ﺓ .ﻙ ﻱ (Harem or Upmarket body warmer).

Visit two or three Santa Clauses to make sure of getting your wishes. If you get two you can always throw one back

Do not use lead weights. Unkind to wildlife. See fishing permits on prohibition of use of lead (law since 1987)

The management of some rivers is excellent, others leave a lot to be desired. This could change either way on privatisation. Anglers should have more say

Fish farming – thoughts of reduced poaching has been a dream. Poaching on some rivers is a local industry

Check water for body and rod shadows. A standing angler is often within a fish's view by refraction

FISHY WOMEN

EVER underestimate women anglers. They can often cast a fly far better than a man, make superb sandwiches and where else can you get such an excellent handwarmer. Don't forget that it is a woman who holds the record for the heaviest rod-caught salmon in Britain. Miss Georgina Ballantine, only 18 years old, caught a 64lb salmon measuring 54 inches long – almost as big as Miss Ballantine herself – girth 28½ inches, head 12 inches, tail 11 inches. Not content with that monster she also had three others weighing 25lb, 21lb and 17lb in the same day.

JEANNIE

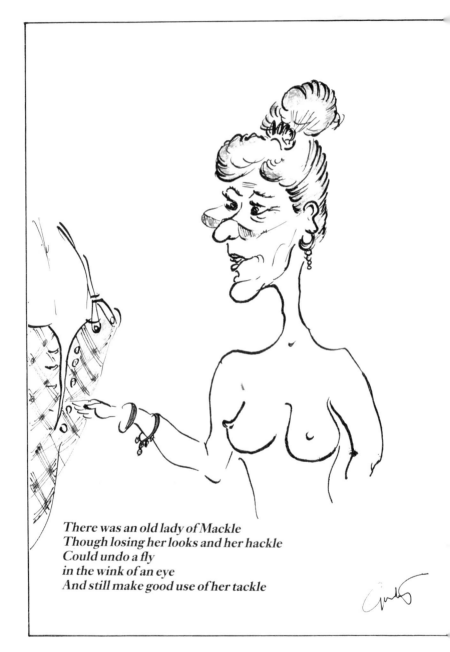

There was an old lady of Mackle
Though losing her looks and her hackle
Could undo a fly
in the wink of an eye
And still make good use of her tackle

When you hand in line fast this is called 'Ripping the Flies'

"IF HER STOCKBROKING IS AS BAD AS HER FISHING LOOK OUT FOR MORE BLACK MONDAYS"

Dress or be prepared for all weathers. Being cold at the waterside can be very miserable and unpleasant

The Twelve Commandments of Salmon Fishing

1. Honour thy bank manager and thy wife that thy days may be long upon the water which the Lord thy owner rented thee.
2. Thou shalt not kill kelts.
3. Thou shalt not commit adultery with mermaids.
4. Thou shalt not steal from the next beat.
5. Thou shalt not bear false witness against thy gillie.
6. Thou shalt not covet thy neighbour's fishing, thou shalt not covet thy fellow fisher's wife, thy neighbour's gillie, nor his wife, nor his dog, nor his life-style, nor anything that is thy brother angler's.
7. Remember the sabbath and keep it for fishing except in Scotland.
8. Six days shalt thou fish and do no work.
9. Ye shall not make lures of gold, neither shall ye make tackle, unless you wish the wrath of thy tackle shop.
10. All the anglers saw the thunderings and the lightnings and the noise of the rain and took to smoking; and when the fish saw it they buggered off afar.
11. Thou shalt not take the name of the Lord thy water owner in vain; for the Lord will not allow him next year that taketh his name in vain.
12. Neither shalt thou go up by steps into deep waters, that thy nakedness be discovered in the fishing hut.

AUTHOR. "McGINTY"

Always double check your boat for tackle and equipment. It can be great fun rowing back 3 miles for your flies

Learn to recognise a kelt. It can be embarrassing on the hotel or hut floor

Don't throw away old broken hooks; very difficult to get out of dogs paws and mermaids

A Page Three girl from out of Montrose
Fished the Esk in her usual pose
The bailies weren't sure
Of such a strange lure
Twas not fish but the anglers that rose

Check what lures are allowed. Some water is fly only, some water allows spinning only on specific height of water

Under certain low water conditions the gillie has to 'back-up' the water – fishing the water upstream

All foul hooked fish should be gently returned to the river, holding the fish
balanced till it swims away

Some gillies are better at teaching it than others

A bunch of flowers is a better buy, especially when three hours late from the fishing on an anniversary

Always drop the point of the rod and take the tension off the fly when a fish is being netted; saves ending up with one eyed gillies, fellow anglers or self

Beware of cheap cottages and caravans to let with access to good fishing.
Check out thoroughly, especially fish catches of the river

Are all fishermen liars? Are all liars fishermen?

You can stay too long at the water. Mermaids and lies should be rested

Stainless steel flasks are magic for broth and soup. Put at top of wedding list

Statistics: Salmon eaten 20% from the sea; 10% from fish farming; 5% from poaching; 1% from rod fishing; 64% from tins

Car phones are better switched off at the water

Red hen fish should always be gently returned to the water – future stock

Youth should be encouraged to fish – never forced

A good sized fish is always worth having professionally mounted – be worth a
fortune to your grandchildren in years to come

Well-Known Gillies' Sayings

You should have been here last week.
You surely have not come here to fish.
The fish don't start running till next week.
It takes a dram or two to catch fish here.
They have gone right off the take.
Too much water, too few fish.
You'll not catch fish if your fly is not in the water.
Can I get the drinks oot of the car for you.
Have you got a smaller fly?
Have you got a bigger fly?
Have you got a lightly dressed fly?
Have you got a heavier dressed fly?
Did you bring any snakes.

Phrases and their meanings – Essential knowledge for fishing in Scotland

YE'LL TOAK A DRAAM – Will you have a drink?
CAW CAANNY WEE DHE WAUTER – Don't put any water in the whisky.
AAM FOO – I am full (only applies to food never drink).
MOARIN – A morning glass of whisky.
AZ DRIIZ A WHASSUL – I am as dry as a whistle or can you open another bottle?
CLAW YOU MII BAAK AALL CLAW YOURZ – See me alright and I fish you through the best lies.
AA NIVVER TAIST – I never taste water.
AA COANAY COMPLEN – I cannot complain (rarely heard).
AA DINNAY KEN – I don't know what's happened to the fish.
SNOW BRUI – The fishing is useless due to snow melting.
DHURZ MOANAY A LEE TELLT AT DHE NEB OA A PEN – There's many a lie told at the point of a pen. (all books on fishing are rubbish).

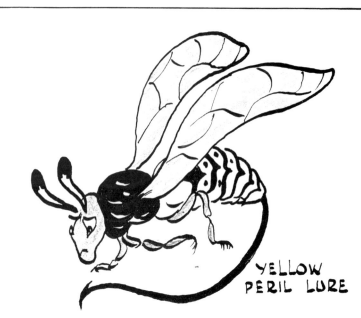

YELLOW
PERIL LURE

A funny old fisher called Lee
Dropped his waders to have a good pee
A wasp stung his willy
And it hurt something silly
But his wife looked at the swelling with glee.

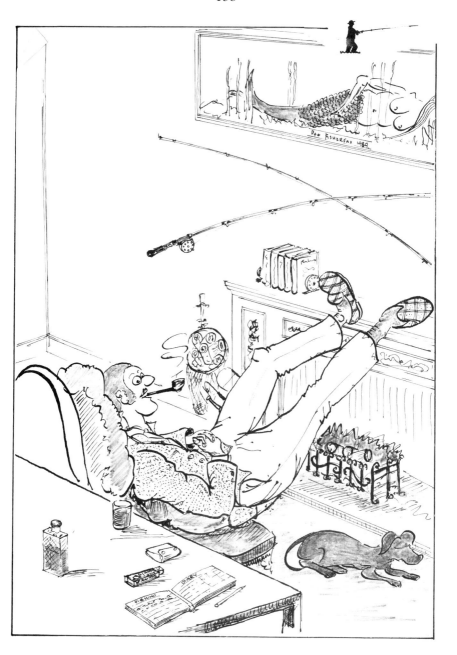

End of a perfect day

GLOSSARY

AFTM	Marketing numbers on a rod stands for A Fortune To Maker.
ALEVIN	Disadvantaged, starts off with the sac.
ANGLING	Something a fisher's wife does not do or understand.
BACKING	The group that supports a reel.
BACKING UP	End of day's fishing.
BAILIFF	Someone paid by result and is always broke.
BAIT	The bread and butter of fishing.
BEACH	Something you can never find when you want one.
BLOODKNOT	Something squeezed out of nylon.
CASTING	Film director's fringe benefit.
CHECK LIST	Something you can never find.
COCK UP	Impossible for male salmon.
DAPPING	Taking only a slight interest in fishing.
DRAG	The ripple caused by a fisher wearing funny clothes.
DROPPER	A device for catching up on everything.
FALSE CAST	An actress that got a job from a couch.
FLIES	Come in two species button and zip.
FRY	Fishing in brilliant sunshine.
GAFF	Known as the Blacksmith's Fly and a joke that should not be used at the water.
GILLIE	Something that requires internal lubrication before working.
GREASED LINE	Talking a gillie into a bribe to fish.
GRILSE	Being all at sea for a year.
HACKLE	Hairs on the neck of a hooked gillie.
HOOKING	Fishing carried out on the River Soho.

HOOKS	Water-letting middle men.
JOCK SCOTT	Name written in hotel register in Scotland like Smith.
KELT	A kind of skirt worn by salmon after sex.
KNOT	Something that sometimes works.
LEADER	Something that never goes where directed.
LURE	Expression on an angler's face.
LIE	The art of fishing story telling.
LANDING NET	Type of curtain used at the top of the stairs.
LATERAL LINE	The plimsol line on a salmon.
LINE	Something shot.
LICE	A form of passport carried for entry into a river system.
NEEDLE KNOT	Acupuncture at the river.
MULTIPLIER	Like an accumulator three way bet on the chance of catching a salmon.
PARR	For the coarse fishers.
PERMIT	Very rarely found at the river.
POACHING	Term never understood in courts and lightly done.
PRAWN	Used in a board fishing game.
PULL	When a fish attempts to take a fly and misses.
ROD	An expensive type of pole or stick.
REEL	Unrehearsed dance from a loose rock band.
REDDS	Russian salmon fishers.
RISE	An unexpected bonus at the water.
SALMON	A type of fish that comes in tins.
SCISSORS	Dance step you do before falling in.
SHRIMP	Small angler.
SMOULT	A fish in training for smoking.
SINK TIP	A fish you have bet on that falls at the first water jump.
STRIKE	Fish that are not on the take.

SWIVEL	Another dance step you do before falling in.
TUBE FLIES	Lines bought in underground tackle shops.
WATER	Something you put in whisky, very occasionally.
WADDINGTON	A fishing game.
WATER SENSE	Getting wet from being upset in a river.
WADING STICK	Sort of truss for giving support.
WADE	Something you do through a fishing book that's boring.
WEIGHT	A variable with a lying multiplying factor of two or three.
WORMS	To keep coming off a hook?
WEATHER	Something anglers are often under especially after a few drams.
WEDLOCK	An anti-leaving device used by anglers' wives.
WEEKEND	The period in an angler's diary from Friday night till Thursday night.
WET DREAM	An erotic dream culminating in netted salmon of 65lb.
WET NURSE	A female gillie.
WHINE	A high pitched cry used as an expression in losing a fish.
WHIP	A fishing Member of Parliament.
WHISKY	The water of life not to be diluted with.
WHISKEY	A U.S.A or Irish drinking joke.
WHORE	A spare taken with you when boat fishing.
WIDOW	A woman whose husband spends much time away pursuing a specified activity like fishing.
X	A certificate often on films or videos shown at angling clubs.
YOGA	A system of exercises to attain liberation for angling.
ZIP	Unfortunately never found in belly waders.
ZONKED	Completely exhausted and intoxicated by the act of angling.

NOTES

NOTES

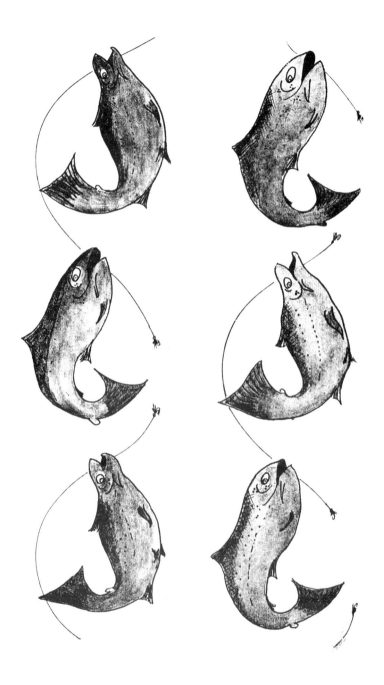